First Person
A ★ M ★ E ★ R ★ I ★ C ★ A

A NATION IS BORN

Rebellion and Independence in America (1700-1820)

Richard Steins

Twenty-First Century Books

A Division of Henry Holt and Company
New York

Twenty-First Century Books
A Division of Henry Holt and Company, Inc.
115 West 18th Street
New York, New York 10011

Henry Holt® and colophon are trademarks of Henry Holt
and Company, Inc.
Publishers since 1866

©1993 by Blackbirch Graphics, Inc.
First Edition
5 4 3 2 1

Published in Canada by Fitzhenry & Whiteside Ltd.
195 Allstate Parkway, Markham, Ontario L3R 4T8

Printed in the United States of America
All first editions are printed on acid-free paper ∞.

Created and produced in association with Blackbirch Graphics, Inc.

Library of Congress Cataloging-in-Publication Data

Steins, Richard.
　　A nation is born: rebellion and independence in America,
　1700–1820 / Richard Steins. — 1st edition.
　　　p.　cm. —(First person America)
　　Includes bibliographical references and index.
　　Summary: Provides primary source materials covering life in the
thirteen colonies, problems with England, the Revolution, and the creation
of the new government of the United States.
　　ISBN 0-8050-2582-0 (alk. paper)
　　1. United States—History—Revolution, 1775–1783—Sources—Juvenile
literature. 2. United States—History—Colonial period, ca. 1600–1775—
Sources—Juvenile literature. 3. United States—History—1783–1815—
Sources—Juvenile literature. [1. United States—History—Colonial period,
ca. 1600–1775—Sources. 2. United States—History—Revolution, 1775–
1783—Sources. 3. United States—History—1783–1815—Sources.] I. Title.
II. Series.
E203.S83　1993
973.3—dc20
　　　　　　　　　　　　　　　　　　　　　　　　　　　　　93-24994
　　　　　　　　　　　　　　　　　　　　　　　　　　　　　CIP
　　　　　　　　　　　　　　　　　　　　　　　　　　　　　AC

CONTENTS

INTRODUCTION

The period between 1700 and 1820 was one of great upheaval as the 13 British colonies in North America revolted against their mother country, established a new nation, and gradually started to expand westward across the continent.

The excerpts that follow give us glimpses of colonial society, politics, and everyday life. We will also read some of the writings of the founders of the new nation—the leaders who first stated the principles on which American government is based. And we will hear the voices of ordinary people who worked to create the nation—the men, women, and children in colonial New England; African Americans brought to North America as slaves; and American Indians—the people who inhabited the land before the arrival of the Europeans.

Shortly before the outbreak of the Revolution in 1775, Great Britain's 13 colonies had helped her in defeating the French—driving them from most of North America. In the conflicts known as the French and Indian Wars, the colonies proved that they could stand on their own. When the British government eventually attempted to control colonial trade and impose taxes that the colonists thought were unfair, rebellion was quick to erupt.

On December 16, 1773, colonists dumped tea into Boston Harbor in what was called the Boston Tea Party (*Library of Congress*).

Colonial society had many different faces. In New England and the Middle Atlantic colonies, the economy was based on trading and small businesses and farms. The South, in contrast, was becoming more and more a plantation economy, which was dependent on slave labor. Despite these differences, the colonies came together to fight—and win—a difficult war against Great Britain, a powerful opponent.

When the British finally surrendered in 1783, the colonies embarked on an experiment in independence. By late 1788 a new Constitution had been adopted, and the American form of government we know today was established. It would not be long before the nation turned its attention to the West—the vast, unexplored area that now makes up part of the United States. With the stroke of a pen and a payment of about

A handwritten page from the original Articles of Confederation (*Library of Congress*).

$15 million, President Thomas Jefferson, in 1803, acquired the Louisiana Purchase from France, which vastly increased the country's territory. To explore this new land, Jefferson sent Lewis and Clark on an expedition across the wilderness—a bold and daring trip that eventually opened the West to American settlers.

In these early voices from America's past we also hear the seeds of disunity and civil war. The brutal conditions described by slaves disturbed many whites, and while the Constitution did not discuss slavery, the question of slavery influenced politics even in these early days. In 1820, a piece of legislation known as the Missouri Compromise was supposed to settle the issue of whether slavery should be allowed in the new territories. But it turned out to be only a temporary solution to a problem that would eventually take an enormous toll in lives and tear the country apart.

CHAPTER 1

EARLY LIFE IN THE COLONIES

The French and Indian Wars

The Europeans who came to what is now the United States in the 1600s and 1700s settled mainly along the eastern seaboard, establishing communities and farms from New England in the North to Georgia in the South. The rest of the vast continent, westward from the coast and extending to the north into what is now Canada, remained largely unsettled by white Europeans. These vast lands were occupied by different groups of Native Americans.

America's unsettled territories became involved in a fierce struggle between Great Britain and France— as the two powers strove for the upper hand in Europe, they also sought control of North America. This struggle was waged on and off between 1689 and 1763, until the French were defeated and lost their North American territories. The various battles that made up this 74-year conflict in the New World are known as the French and Indian Wars.

General James Wolfe died on the Plains of Abraham in Quebec during the French and Indian Wars. Steel engraving by John Sartain (*Library of Congress*).

Both the French and the British tried to control and use the Indians as allies at various times over the long war. The French and Indian Wars were fought along the St. Lawrence River in Canada, in the lake country of what is now northeastern New York State, and at isolated forts in the interior of the continent.

The battle that determined the outcome of the French and Indian Wars was fought on the Plains of Abraham, near Quebec City, Canada, in 1759. British forces under the command of the brilliant and youthful General James Wolfe (1727–1759) fought against

French forces under the leadership of Louis-Joseph de Montcalm (1712–1759). Both Wolfe and Montcalm were killed on the Plains of Abraham. In the end, the French lost the battle and the war. In 1763, the Treaty of Paris ended French control of Canada, which then came under the governing powers of the British.

The French and Indian Wars had a great deal of significance for the 13 colonies. Although the colonists had fought on the side of Britain, of which they were a part, they had shown themselves that they could be self-sufficient in times of crisis. The French and Indian Wars helped to create a greater sense of the colonists as particularly "American" and enabled them to think of themselves for the first time as more than subjects of the British crown.

One of the most famous military commanders toward the end of the French and Indian Wars was Major Robert Rogers (1731–1795), a British colonial soldier, who commanded a group known as Rogers' Rangers. Their mission was to raid and destroy French and Indian encampments and drive the enemy from the region near Lake George, New York.

The following excerpt is from Rogers' journal. It describes a mission to spy on French forces near Lake George. By the end of the 1750s, the French forces were already losing ground in the struggle. A French fort located in western Pennsylvania, called Fort Duquesne, had been built by Virginians in 1754, but they were driven out by the French that same year. As their military situation worsened, the French abandoned the fort, and it was taken over by the British and promptly renamed Fort Pitt. The city of Pittsburgh is on the site of the old Fort Pitt and takes its name from that structure.

The Journal of Major Rogers

We advanced half a mile over broken ground, passed a valley of fifteen rods breadth, when the front having gained the summit of the opposite hill on the west side, fell in with the enemy drawn up in the form of a crescent to surround us, and were immediately saluted with a volley of 200 shot, at a distance of five yards from the nearest, and thirty yards from the rear of the party. This fire took place about 2 o'clock P.M. and proved fatal to Lieut. Kennedy, and Mr. Gardner a volunteer, besides wounding several, and myself in the head. I ordered my men to retire to the opposite hill, where Lieut. Stark and Mr. Brewer had made a stand with forty men to cover our retreat. We were closely pursued—Capt. Spikeman and others were killed and several made prisoners. Lieut. Stark repulsed them by a brisk fire from the hill, killing a number, and affording us an opportunity to post ourselves to advantage. Mr. Stark then took a position in the centre, with Ensign Rogers; sergeants Walker and Phillips acting as reserves, to protect our flanks, and watch the enemy's motions. Soon after, we had thus formed for battle, the enemy attempted to flank us; but the reserve bravely attacked them, giving the first fire, which stopped several from retreating to the main body....

We kept up a constant fire until sunset, when I received a shot through my wrist, which disabled me from loading my gun. The action however continued until darkness prevented our seeing each other. Our men gallantly kept their position till the fire of the enemy ceased and he retired.

From: *Reminiscences of the French War with Robert Rogers' Journal and a Memoir of General Stark* (Concord, New Hampshire: Luther Roby, 1831).

The Harsh Life of a Slave

About 35 million Americans of black-African descent live in the United States today. Almost all are descendants of slaves who were brought to North and South America and the West Indies from West Africa.

The first slaves arrived in Jamestown and the other British colonies of North America as early as 1619, shortly after the first white European settlers arrived. They were brought to the New World as agricultural laborers, to work raising coffee, tobacco, sugar, and rice. Only in the 1700s and 1800s were they used in the United States on the cotton plantations that flourished in the South.

During colonial times, ships would set sail for West Africa, carrying cargoes of manufactured goods that had been produced in the factories of Europe. Off the coast of West Africa the white traders would barter their goods for black slaves, who were most often traded by other black Africans. The slaves were crammed onto the ships that had just unloaded their goods to begin a journey of six to eight weeks across the Atlantic Ocean to the West Indies or to North or South America.

In the New World, the human cargo that had survived the trip was unloaded and put up for sale to slave buyers. The ships then took on agricultural products, for example, coffee, sugar, and rice, and returned to Europe. This method of trading brought

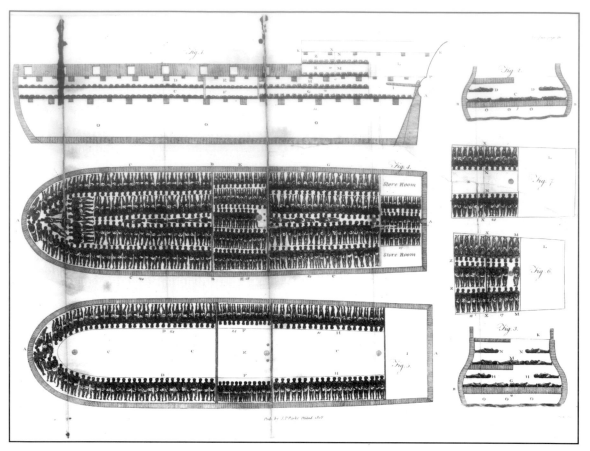

This illustration shows how slaves were packed into ships for their long journey to the New World (*Library of Congress*).

hundreds of thousands of black-African slaves to the New World for almost 200 years.

There are practically no first-person accounts from slaves themselves about the trip from West Africa to the Americas. One that does survive is by an African who came to be called Gustavus Vasa and who was shipped as a slave to the New World in 1756. His account of the hardships of the "middle passage," as the trip from Africa was called, was published in Great Britain in 1793 after he had won his freedom and gone to England.

There are no surviving records of how many slaves died before reaching the New World. Many perished resisting their captors before even boarding the ships. Others died of disease in the terrible conditions on the vessels, and some even committed suicide rather than submit to slavery. If smallpox broke out on board the ship, sick and some healthy slaves were often thrown overboard to prevent the disease from spreading.

The slave trade was not officially abolished in the United States until 1808, almost 20 years after the adoption of the U.S. Constitution. By the time the American Civil War broke out in 1861, about 4 million Americans—1 out of every 8—were black-African descendants of those who had survived the trip in captivity from West Africa.

Slaves work on a Southern tobacco plantation in the early 1800s (*Library of Congress*).

The following excerpt, which describes the harsh conditions of captivity, is from the personal account of Gustavus Vasa.

The Account of Gustavus Vasa

The stench of the hold while we were on the coast, was so intolerably loathsome, that it was dangerous to remain there for any time, and some of us had been permitted to stay on the deck for the fresh air; but now that the whole ship's cargo were confined together, it became absolutely pestilential. The closeness of the place, and the heat of the climate, to the number in the ship, which was so crowded that each had scarcely room to turn himself, almost suffocated us....

The shrieks of the women, and the groans of the dying, rendered the whole a scene of horror almost inconceivable. Happily perhaps for myself, I was soon reduced so low here that it was thought necessary to keep me almost always on deck; and from my extreme youth I was not put in fetters. In this situation I expected every hour to share the fate of my companions some of whom were almost daily brought upon deck at the point of which I began to hope would soon put an end to my miseries.

From: *The Interesting Narrative of the Life of Olandah Eguiano or Gustavus Vasa, Written by Himself* (London:1793).

Social Commentary from Poor Richard

Benjamin Franklin. Color aquatint by Pierre Michel Alix (*National Portrait Gallery*).

Benjamin Franklin (1706–1790) was a great American statesman, printer, scientist, and writer. He was born in Boston, the son of a soap-maker. At the age of 10 he left school to work with his father. By 1723, at the age of 17, he moved to Philadelphia to work as a printer.

After a short stay in England, Franklin returned to Philadelphia. By 1730 he had become the owner and editor of the newspaper the *Pennsylvania Gazette*. His writings brought him fame, and in 1732 he began to publish *Poor Richard's Almanack*, an enormously successful "magazine" of the day, which he published and revised every year until 1757.

Poor Richard was a fictional character who dispensed advice on common sense and honesty, traits that Franklin firmly believed in. Many of Poor Richard's proverbs have become part of American folklore. Two of the most famous are, "God helps them that help themselves," and "Early to bed, and early to rise, makes a man healthy, wealthy, and wise."

Franklin's many contributions as a statesman, writer, and scientist have earned him lasting fame as one of the great early Americans.

The following selections are from various issues of *Poor Richard's Almanack* that were published between 1736 and 1746. The first is a playful poem about the identity of Poor Richard; the others are witty phrases and sayings that were quoted by many of the colonists every day.

A page from *Poor Richard's Almanack* (*Library of Congress*).

From *Poor Richard's Almanack*

Who is Poor Richard? People oft enquire,
Where lives? What is he?—never yet the nigher.
Somewhat to ease your Curiositie,
Take these slight Sketches of my Dame and me.
Thanks to kind Readers and careful Wife,
With plenty bles'd, I lead an easy Life;
My Business Writing; her to drain the Mead,
Or crown the barren Hill with useful Shade;
In the Smooth Glebe to see the Plowshare worn,
And fill the Granary with needful Corn.
Press nectarous Cyder from my loaded Trees,
Print the sweet butter, turn the drying Cheese.
Some books we read, tho' few there are that hit
The happy Point where wisdom joins with Wit;
That set fair virtue naked to our View,
And teach us what is *decent*, what is *true*.

A good wife and health
Is a man's best wealth.

A quarrelsome man
has no good neighbours.

Three things are men most liable
to be cheated in,
a Horse, a Wig, and a Wife.

He that scatters thorns,
let him not go barefoot.

God heals
and the Doctor takes the fees.

If you desire many things,
many things will seem but a few.

Mary's mouth costs her nothing,
for she never opens it but at others expence.

From: *Poor Richard's Almanack* by Benjamin Franklin, various
editions from 1736–1746 (Philadelphia).

CHAPTER 2

REBELLION
AND
REVOLUTION

First Reactions to a "Declaration"

In the colonies, the idea of separation from Great Britain was one that at first developed slowly, then accelerated rather quickly. Less than 20 years before the Revolutionary War, the colonists had supported the British in their struggle against the French in North America.

But by the 1760s, the colonists' grievances against Britain had grown to such a degree that even Benjamin Franklin—a moderate by most standards—was considering the possibility of independence. In July 1775, Franklin had proposed that the colonies unite and form a confederation. A prominent statesman and delegate from Virginia, Thomas Jefferson (1743–1826), made notes of Franklin's proposals, and used them while writing his Declaration of Independence.

The handwritten version of the Declaration of Independence (*National Archives*).

Just a year later, on June 7, 1776, Richard Henry Lee (1732–1794), a delegate to the Second Continental Congress from Virginia, suggested a resolution that called for independence from Great Britain. A few days later, the Congress appointed five delegates to prepare a statement giving reasons for independence. John Adams (1735–1826), a delegate from Massachusetts, and Thomas Jefferson were appointed to write the statement.

Jefferson felt Adams should write the draft, but Adams stubbornly refused, saying that he was disliked by the other delegates and that his lack of popularity would affect the way the statement would be received. According to Adams, Jefferson was the better writer.

Jefferson wrote the Declaration of Independence, and Adams and Benjamin Franklin made minor changes in wording. On July 2, 1776, the Congress accepted Lee's resolution calling for independence, and on July 4, 1776, the delegates adopted the Declaration. From then on, July 4 became the day on which America celebrated her independence.

The Declaration of Independence stated that the American Revolution was more than a simple rebellion. It was an attempt to establish a government based on the consent of the people governed, not on force. And it was a government based on the basic rights of its citizens.

The ideas set forth in the Declaration today sound as true and familiar to Americans as the national anthem. But in 1776, the text of the Declaration was considered quite bold and innovative. For people who had lived so long under the rule of England—people who, to a great extent, still considered themselves English—the idea of declaring independence was a severe and even frightening one.

After the Declaration was adopted, it was read publicly in major cities throughout the colonies. Though

The final, approved version of the Declaration of Independence was signed in Philadelphia on July 4, 1776. This famous painting was done by John Trumbull (*National Archives*).

not everyone agreed with its stand, the majority of the colonists welcomed the Declaration. The following excerpt contains personal recollections of colonists who heard the Declaration of Independence being read for the first time. The passage describes a general atmosphere of great celebration and a newly born sense of national pride in people who, in many ways, had just become "newly born" Americans.

The People Respond

JULY 8.—At twelve o'clock to-day, the Committees of Safety and Inspection of Philadelphia, went in procession to the State House, where the Declaration of the Independency of the United States of America was read to a very large number of the inhabitants of the city and county, and was received with general applause and heartfelt satisfaction. And, in the evening, our late king's coat-of-arms was brought from the hall in the State House, where the said king's courts were formerly held, and burned amidst the acclamations of a crowd of spectators.

The Declaration was received at Easton, in Pennsylvania, and proclaimed in the following order:—The Colonel and all the other field officers of the first battalion repaired to the court-house, the light infantry company marching there with their drums beating, fifes playing, and the standard, (the device for which is the Thirteen United Colonies,) which was ordered to be displayed. After that the Declaration was read aloud to a great number of spectators, who gave their hearty assent with three loud huzzas, and cried out, "May God long preserve and unite the FREE and INDEPENDENT States of America."

From: *Diary of the American Revolution,* Vol. 1, by Frank Moore (New York: Charles Scribner's Sons, 1858).

The Influence of Thomas Paine

Thomas Paine. Mezzotint by James Watson (*National Portrait Gallery*).

Today we live in a time of instant news. Through television's use of satellites orbiting above the earth, we are able to learn of, and see, events even as they occur.

In colonial America, information traveled slowly, and it was transmitted by one principal means, the printed word. A pamphlet that was printed in Boston or Philadelphia, for example, would take several weeks to reach Georgia, because horseback was the only way of transporting it. There were no telephones or telegraphs, no televisions or radios.

Because the printed word was the only way that ideas could be communicated over great distances, books, newspapers, and pamphlets took on great significance. People who had the gift of writing well gained great prominence and influence.

Thomas Paine (1737–1809), a well-known writer and political thinker, was a strong supporter of the American Revolution. His works were widely read in the colonies and abroad, and their popularity did much to justify the cause of the colonists and to encourage them in their struggle for independence.

Paine was born in England of Quaker parents. He met Benjamin Franklin when Franklin was in London in the 1770s, and with letters of introduction from the American, Paine moved to the colonies and began to write in support of the Revolution.

COMMON SENSE;

ADDRESSED TO THE

INHABITANTS

O F

A M E R I C A,

On the following interesting

S U B J E C T S.

I. Of the Origin and Design of Government in general,
with concise Remarks on the English Constitution.

II. Of Monarchy and Hereditary Succession.

III. Thoughts on the present State of American Affairs.

IV. Of the present Ability of America, with some mis-
cellaneous Reflections.

Man knows no Master save creating HEAVEN,
Or those whom choice and common good ordain.

THOMSON.

PHILADELPHIA;

Printed, and Sold, by R. BELL, in Third-Street.

MDCCLXXVI.

The original printed title page from Thomas Paine's *Common Sense,* published in 1776 (*Library of Congress*).

One of Paine's most popular pamphlets was *Common Sense,* which was published in January 1776. In the excerpt printed here, Paine argues that the colonies had outgrown their relationship with Great Britain and would prosper if they were independent.

In later years, Paine's antigovernment writings and activities alienated many people in America, and he was shunned by a number of influential individuals. He died in poverty.

Paine held no public office, yet his words inspired people and moved them to action. In many ways, Paine served as the Revolution's morale booster—its cheerleader, constantly reminding the colonists of the courageousness of their efforts.

Paine was an exciting writer. He was widely read, and although his ideas did not reach the lofty, oratorical tone of Thomas Jefferson or the cool and reasoned argument of James Madison (1751–1836), they did contain fire and passion. They defined the ideas that inspired the fighters of the revolution and conveyed the hopes that united pro-independence forces throughout the 13 colonies. If the colonists had not been so inspired in their cause, the outcome of the war for independence—and indeed, of our history—could have been very different.

From *Common Sense*

I have heard it asserted by some, that as America has flourished under her former connection with Great Britain, the same connection is necessary towards her future happiness, and will always have the same effect. Nothing can be more fallacious than this kind of argument. We may as well assert that because a child has thrived upon milk, that it is never to have meat, or that the first twenty years of our lives is to become a precedent for the next twenty. But even this is admitting more than is true; for I answer roundly, that America would have flourished as much, and probably much more, had no European power taken any notice of her. The commerce by which she hath enriched herself are the necessaries of life, and will always have a market while eating is the custom of Europe.

But she has protected us, say some. That she hath engrossed us is true, and defended the continent at our expense as well as her own, is admitted; and she would have defended Turkey from the same motive, *viz.* for the sake of trade and dominion.

Alas! we have been long led away by ancient prejudices and made large sacrifices to superstition. We have boasted the protection of Great Britain, without considering, that her motive was *interest* not *attachment*; and that she did not protect us from *our enemies* on *our account*; but from her *enemies* on *her own account*, from those who had no quarrel with us on any *other account*, and who will always be our enemies on the same account. Let Britain waive her pretensions to the continent, or the continent throw off the dependence, and we should be at peace with France and Spain, were they at war with Britain.

From: *Common Sense* by Thomas Paine (Philadelphia: R. Bell, 1776).

"Remember the Ladies"

Women played a significant role in the American Revolution. Although they did not enjoy the same political and property rights that men did—in fact, they were kept subservient to men in all phases of life—colonial women supported the Revolution with the same degree of patriotism and fervor. As farmers, housekeepers, and mothers, they did not only the work that was expected of them, but in many cases they also took up the work of absent men who had volunteered to serve in the Continental Army.

John Adams. Oil portrait by John Trumbull (*National Portrait Gallery*).

Women did not receive the right to vote in the United States until early in the twentieth century. But the call for women's rights existed as far back as the Revolution. One of the most outspoken advocates of equality for women was Abigail Smith Adams (1744–1818), the wife of John Adams, a leader of the American Revolution and later the second president of the United States.

The letters of John and Abigail Adams excerpted here were written in the spring of 1776, just a few months before the Declaration of Independence was adopted. Abigail, knowing the colonists would be seeking independence, writes in a partly serious, partly joking way, warning her husband to "Remember the Ladies." She teases him by saying that "All Men would be tyrants if they could," and that women might start a rebellion if their rights are not considered.

John replies, partly in jest, that the Revolution has already caused the loss of government authority everywhere and that men will never undo the "Masculine systems" but would exercise power gently and with caution.

Beneath the jesting tone of the letters, however, lay very serious issues that would confront the new nation for years to come. Women's rights were not written into the new Constitution, and not until

Abigail Adams. Engraving by S. A. Schoff (*Library of Congress*).

1920 did the states finally approve a Constitutional amendment that granted women the right to vote. In more recent times, the states failed to pass the "Equal Rights Amendment" (ERA), which stated simply that any discrimination based on gender was unconstitutional.

Abigail Adams probably had no idea that many of the rights and protections she advocated in the 1770s would still be a subject of debate 200 years later. Nevertheless, with the ear of one of the most powerful men in government so easily accessible, Abigail took the opportunity to make the case for equality in the new nation.

Abigail Adams to John Adams—
March 31, 1776

I long to hear that you have declared an independency—and by the way in the new Code of Laws which I suppose it will be necessary for you to make I desire you would Remember the Ladies, and be more generous and favourable to them than your ancestors. Do not put such unlimited power into the hands of the Husbands. Remember all Men would be tyrants if they could. If perticuliar care and attention is not paid to the Laidies we are determined to foment a Rebelion, and will not hold ourselves bound by any Laws in which we have no voice, or Representation.

That your Sex are Naturally Tyrannical is a Truth so thoroughly established as to admit of no dispute, but such of you as wish to be happy willingly give up the harsh title of Master for the more tender and endearing one of Friend. Why then, not put it out of the power of the vicious and the Lawless to use us with cruelty and indignity with impunity. Men of Sense in all Ages abhor those customs which treat us only as the vassals of your Sex. Regard us then as Being placed by providence under your protection and in immitation of the Supreme Being make use of that power only for our happiness.

From: *Familiar Letters of John Adams and His Wife Abigail During the Revolution* (New York: Hurd and Houghton, 1876).

John Adams to Abigail Adams—April 14, 1776

As to Declarations of Independency, be patient. Read our Privateering Laws, and our Commercial Laws. What signifies a Word.

As to your extraordinary Code of Laws, I cannot but laugh. We have been told that our Struggle has loosened the bands of Government every where. That Children and Apprentices were disobedient—that schools and Colledges were grown turbulent—that Indians slighted their Guardians and Negroes grew insolent to their Masters. But your Letter was the first Intimation that another Tribe more numerous and powerfull than all the rest were grown discontented.—This is rather too coarse a Compliment but you are so saucy, I wont blot it out.

Depend upon it, We know better than to repeal our Masculine systems. Altho they are in full Force, you know they are little more than Theory. We dare not exert our Power in its full Latitude. We are obliged to go fair, and softly, and in Practice you know We are the subjects. We have only the Name of Masters, and rather than give up this, which would compleatly subject Us to the Despotism of the Peticoat, I hope General Washington, and all our brave Heroes would fight. I am sure every good Politician would plot, as long as he would against Despotism, Empire, Monarchy, Aristocracy, Oligarchy, or Ochlocracy.—A fine Story indeed. I begin to think the Ministry as deep as they are wicked. After stirring up Tories, Landjobbers, Trimmers, Bigots, Canadians, Indians, Negroes, Hanoverians, Hessians, Russians, Irish Roman Catholicks, Scotch Renegadoes, at last they have stimulated the people to demand new Priviledges and threaten to rebell.

From: *Familiar Letters of John Adams and His Wife Abigail During the Revolution* (New York: Hurd and Houghton, 1876).

CHAPTER 3

LIFE IN THE NEW COUNTRY

Captured by Indians

In the 1740s, what is now New York State was a colony of Great Britain. White settlers had gradually moved into the western part of the colony, which was also the home of a number of American Indian tribes.

The colonists and the Indians frequently fought each other. The white settlers, who wanted to farm the land, brought with them European customs and religion. The Indians had lived on the land first and were mainly hunters and trappers.

The wars between the Indians and the settlers took many lives and were often very brutal. In 1755, a 12-year-old girl named Mary Jemison, whose family had migrated to western New York, was captured along with several other settlers by a group of Indians.

A few of the captives were eventually returned to their families. Others disappeared altogether. But Mary was given to two Seneca Indian sisters whose brother had been killed the year before in a battle with white settlers. It was Seneca custom to give a captured prisoner to a family who had lost a son or father in battle.

The Seneca sisters regarded Mary as their new "sister" and adopted her in a Seneca ceremony. They dressed her as an Indian and taught her Indian customs and language. Mary missed her parents terribly. She eventually married a Seneca Indian and had children who were raised as Indians.

For the rest of her long life, Mary lived among the Seneca. She never learned to read or write English. In 1823, at the age of 80, Mary was interviewed by Dr. James Seaver, who asked her to describe her life as a "white woman among the Indians." Her story was first published in 1824 and has been republished in many editions since then.

The Indians of the northeastern United States had highly organized societies and lived peacefully among themselves for generations before European settlers arrived in North America. Oil painting by Seth Eastman (*Architect of the Capitol*).

In the passage printed here, Mary describes what daily life was like for a Seneca woman. She remembers her adopted people with great love. Her picture of life among the Seneca was a powerful contradiction to the white people's image of the "savage" Indian.

Recollections of a "White Indian"

In the summer season, we planted, tended and harvested our corn, and generally had all our children with us; but had no master to oversee or drive us, so that we could work as leisurely as we pleased. We had no ploughs on the Ohio; but performed the whole process of planting and hoeing with a small tool that resembled, in some respects, a hoe with a very short handle.

Our cooking consisted in pounding our corn into samp or hommany,* boiling the hommany, making now and then a cake and baking it in the ashes, and in boiling or roasting our venison. As our cooking and eating utensils consisted of a hommany block and pestle, a small kettle, a knife or two, and a few vessels of bark or wood, it required but little time to keep them in order for use.

Spinning, weaving, sewing, stocking knitting, and the like, are arts which have never been practised in the Indian tribes generally. After the revolutionary war, I learned to sew, so that I could make my own clothing after a poor fashion; but the other domestic arts I have been wholly ignorant of the application of, since my captivity. In the season

*Hominy (hommany) is shucked corn with the germ removed; samp is a boiled cereal made from hominy.

of hunting, it was our business, in addition to our cooking, to bring home the game that was taken by the Indians, dress it, and carefully preserve the eatable meat, and prepare or dress the skins. Our clothing was fastened together with strings of deer skin, and tied on with the same.

In that manner we lived, without any of those jealousies, quarrels, and revengeful battles between families and individuals, which have been common in the Indian tribes since the introduction of ardent spirits* amongst them.

The use of ardent spirits amongst the Indians, and the attempts which have been made to civilize and christianize them by the white people, has constantly made them worse and worse; increased their vices, and robbed them of many of their virtues; and will ultimately produce their extermination. I have seen, in a number of instances, the effects of education upon some of our Indians, who were taken when young, from their families, and placed at school before they had had an opportunity to contract many Indian habits, and there kept till they arrived to manhood; but I have never seen one of those but what was an Indian in every respect after he returned. Indians must and will be Indians, in spite of all the means that can be used for their cultivation in the sciences and arts.

*Ardent spirits was a term for alcohol, or liquor.

From: *A Narrative of the Life of Mary Jemison; Deh-He-Wa-Mis* by Dr. James Seaver (New York: Miller, Orton, and Mulligan, 1856).

No Freedom for Slaves

The promise of freedom and opportunity that lured so many Europeans to colonial America was not shared by early African-American settlers. Their ancestors had been brought to the colonies against their will—as slaves from West Africa.

Slavery existed in all of the colonies, but it gradually began to die out in the northeast, especially in New England. The northeast was a hard and cold land, a place of small farms and shops, of cities filled with merchants, traders, and fishermen. Slavery was more suited to the agriculturally based South, where the climate was warmer and large tracts of plantation land were gradually given over to cotton, rice, and tobacco farming.

Indentured servants most often worked for someone only until their debt was paid off. They lost their freedom only temporarily. For black slaves, however, there was no hope of freedom—ever. Slaves could be bought and sold. They could be separated forever from their husbands, wives, children, and parents. They would work from dawn until dusk for no pay. If they tried to escape, they could be forcibly returned to their masters, and they could be beaten and punished in any way the master saw fit. Slaves were treated not as human beings, but as property.

Much has been written about the history of slavery in America, but very little of it has come directly from the slaves themselves. Because most slaves were denied any education, few of them learned to read or write. There are only a handful of surviving letters written by slaves in the 1700s.

The letter printed here provides historians with a rare glimpse of the actual thoughts and feelings of a slave in colonial America. The author is a woman named Judith Cocks, who has been moved from New England to Georgia and separated from her children. This letter is printed exactly in the way Judith Cocks originally wrote it, addressed to a white slave owner named James Hillhouse. It may seem hard to read at first, because she could not spell well, and she did not know grammar and punctuation. But her cry of anguish and concern for her children shines through as she expresses her fondest wish to see them again someday.

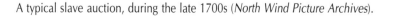

A typical slave auction, during the late 1700s (*North Wind Picture Archives*).

Judith Cocks raises only one voice of pain and sorrow, but she speaks to today's readers for a silent and lost generation of African Americans who, as slaves, helped to build America.

Judith Cocks to James Hillhouse
Marietta, 8th March 1795

Sir

I have been so unhappy at Mrs. Woodbridges that I was obliged to leeve thare by the consent of Mrs. Woodbridge who gave up my Indentures and has offen said that had she known that I was so sickly and expencieve she would not have brought me to this Country but all this is the least of my trouble and I can truly say sir had I nothing else or no one but myself I am sure I should not make any complaint to you But my Little son Jupiter who is now with Mrs. Woodbridge is my greatest care and from what she says and from the useage he meets with there is so trying to me that I am all most distracted therefore if you will be so kind as to write me how Long Jupiter is to remain with them as she tells me he is to live with her untill he is twenty five years of age this is something that I had no idea of I all ways thought that he was to return with me to new england or at Longest only ten years these are matters I must beg of you sir to let me know as quick as you can make it convenient I hope you will excuse me of troub Ling you wich I think you will do when you think that I am here in A strange country without one Friend to advise me Mrs. Woodbridge setts out for connecticut and I make

no doubt but she will apply to buy Jupiter's time
which I beg you will be so good as not to sell to her
I had much reather he wold return and Live with
you as she allows all her sons to thump and beat
him the same as if he was a Dog Mrs. Woodbridge
may tell you that I have behaved bad but I call on all
the nabours to known wheather I have not behaved
well and wheather I was so much to blame She has
called me A thief and I denie I have don my duty as
well as I could to her and all her family as well as
my Strength wold allow of I have not ronged her
nor her family the nabours advised me to rite you for
the childs sake I went to the Gentlemen of the town
for these advise they told me I could get back without any difficulty I entend to return remember me
to all your family if you please I thank you for
sending me word my daughter was well this is my
hand writing I remain the greatest humility[,] you
Humble servant

Judith Cocks

please [don't?] show this to Mrs. Woodbridge

From: *Slave Testimony: Two Centuries of Letters, Speeches, Inter-
views, and Autobiographies,* John W. Blassingame, ed. (Baton Rouge,
Louisiana: Louisiana State University Press, 1977). Copyright © 1977
by Louisiana State University Press. Reprinted by permission.

Ravaged by an Epidemic

Philadelphia, Pennsylvania, is one of the largest cities in the United States today, with a population of more than 1.5 million. It is also a great historic city, the site of the signing of the Declaration of Independence and the Continental Congress that was formed early in our country's history. From 1790 to 1800, Philadelphia was the capital of the United States. In 1796, a Philadelphia newspaper published President George Washington's (1732–1799) famous farewell address to the nation.

It may seem hard to believe that in the 1790s the population of Philadelphia was only around 55,000. Yet, for its time, it was a large city. Today, people who live in cities take many things for granted. Their garbage is collected, they have sewers to drain off rainwater and waste material, there are police officers to protect them from criminals, and there are fire fighters to put out fires. When people are sick, they have hospitals in their communities and doctors to care for them until they have recovered.

But imagine life in colonial cities, where many of these services did not exist. Philadelphia's population then was small compared with its present size. But it was still a crowded city, with people bunched together in small houses mostly made of wood. Modern fire-fighting equipment did not exist. Every fire could potentially burn down many blocks of homes. Garbage piled up in the streets, which were populated not only by people but also by horses and chickens.

A bustling market scene on the corner of Third and Market streets, Philadelphia, around 1795. Engraving by W. Birch and Son (*Library of Congress*).

Under such poor sanitary conditions, many kinds of illnesses frequently broke out. Some of these communicable diseases struck down hundreds and even thousands of people. Most of these illnesses are ones that we never or rarely see today in the United States: cholera, smallpox, and yellow fever.

In 1793, Philadelphia suffered a severe outbreak of yellow fever, an infectious disease transmitted by mosquitoes living in stagnant pools of water. Doctors had no idea what caused the disease or how to treat it. The excerpt printed here, written as a firsthand account by a fictitious character but based on actual historical data and the personal experiences of the author, offers a graphic and disturbing picture of the conditions in Philadelphia during the epidemic.

Today, with modern sanitation and with advances in medicine, yellow fever no longer threatens life in our cities. In colonial times, however, this fatal disease was a nightmare that could strike at any time—a deadly disease the colonists were powerless to fight.

Images of the Year 1793

I lay upon a mattress, whose condition proved that a half-decayed corpse had recently been dragged from it. The room was large, but it was covered with beds like my own. Between each, there was scarcely the interval of three feet. Each sustained a wretch, whose groans and distortions bespoke the desperateness of his condition.

The atmosphere was loaded by mortal stenches. A vapour, suffocating and malignant, scarcely allowed me to breathe. No suitable receptacle was provided for the evacuations produced by medicine or disease. My nearest neighbour was struggling with death, and my bed, casually extended, was moist with the detestable matter which had flowed from his stomach.

You will scarcely believe that, in this scene of horrors, the sound of laughter should be overheard. While the upper rooms of this building are filled with the sick and the dying, the lower apartments are the scene of carousals and mirth. The wretches who are hired, at enormous wages, to tend the sick and convey away the dead, neglect their duty, and consume the cordials which are provided for the patients, in debauchery and riot.

From: *Arthur Mervyn*, Vol. 1, by Charles Brockden Brown (Philadelphia: David McKay Publishers, 1887).

CHAPTER 4

A GOVERNMENT IS FORMED

Questioning the Constitution

The Constitution of the United States is the document that created our current American government and described the principles on which it is based. It was written by 55 delegates who gathered during the sweltering summer of 1787 at the Constitutional Convention in Philadelphia. It was signed on September 17, 1787. Before it could go into effect, it needed to be ratified by at least 9 of the original 13 states. Ratification occurred by June 21, 1788, at which time the Constitution replaced the Articles of Confederation, the first rules of government established in America after the American Revolution.

The Articles of Confederation gave many powers to the states and few to the central government. States, for example, could place tariffs on commerce from one state to another. As a result, a strong national economy could not develop.

The Constitution was a compromise between those who favored strong states' rights and those who wanted a strong federal government. (Little was known about the actual day-to-day deliberations of the convention until 1840, when James Madison's notes were first published.) Until late June, the delegates had been quarreling about how power would be distributed between the large states and the small states.

The "Great Compromise," proposed by Connecticut delegate Roger Sherman (1721–1793), suggested a two-house Congress—a House of Representatives, where state delegations would be proportional in size to a state's population, and a Senate, where each state would have two representatives regardless of its size.

The original handwritten draft of the Constitution of the United States (*National Archives*).

The Constitution barely mentions the divisive issue of slavery. The compromise over slavery resulted in counting each slave as three fifths of a person in determining representation in the House of Representatives.

The Constitution is a fairly short document that begins with a Preamble that describes the source of the powers conferred by the rest of the Constitution ("We the People...."). It also contains 7 articles that set up the Congress, the presidency, and the court system and describe the relationship between these bodies and the states; and the 27 amendments that have been added since the Constitution went into effect.

Many people believe that the strength of the Constitution rests on the fact that it *is* such a short document. Because it describes the principles of the American government in such general terms, the Constitution has been reinterpreted to adapt to changing circumstances—it has grown and changed as America has evolved. The specific powers of government that are described in the Constitution are known as the "enumerated" powers. Those not specifically described but assumed to be inherent in the principles of the Constitution are known as the "implied" powers. For example, the Constitution does not establish the power of the Supreme Court to review the constitutionality of laws passed by the Congress. But in 1803, in the case of *Marbury* v. *Madison*, the Court assumed "implied" power. Since then, the Constitution may be said to mean what the Court says it means, and "judicial review" has become an established part of the American system of government.

The selection that follows—a speech by Patrick Henry (1736–1799) on the floor of the Virginia Convention of 1788 that was convened to discuss ratification of the Constitution—provides a firsthand look at some of the discussion that surrounded the adoption of the Constitution. Henry was strongly opposed to an all-powerful central government and argued that the proposed Constitution would create a government that could abuse its people just as Britain had abused the colonies. Although his argument was eloquent and impassioned, Henry failed to persuade his fellow delegates to block the passage of the Constitution.

Patrick Henry (*North Wind Picture Archives*).

Patrick Henry on Democracy

My great objection to this government is, that it does not leave us the means of defending our rights; or, of waging war against tyrants. It is urged by some gentlemen, that this new plan will bring us an acquisition of strength, an army, and the militia of the states. This is an idea extremely ridiculous: gentlemen cannot be in earnest. This acquisition will trample on your fallen liberty. Let my beloved Americans guard against that fatal lethargy that has pervaded the universe. Have we the means of resisting disciplined armies, when our only defence, the militia, is put into the hands of congress?...

However uncharitable it may appear, yet I must tell my opinion, that the most unworthy characters may get into power and prevent the introduction of amendments. Let us suppose (for the case is suppos-able, possible, and probable) that you happen to deal these powers to unworthy hands; will they relinquish powers already in their possession, or, agree to amendments? Two-thirds of the congress, or, of the state legislatures, are necessary even to propose amendments. If one-third of these be unworthy men, they may prevent the application for amendments; but what is destructive and mischie-vous is, that three-fourths of the state legislatures, or of state conventions, must concur in the amend-ments when proposed: in such numerous bodies, there must necessarily be some designing bad men. To suppose that so large a number as three-fourths of the states will concur, is to suppose that they will possess genius, intelligence, and integrity, approach-ing to miraculous. It would indeed be miraculous that they should concur in the same amendments, or, even in such as would bear some likeness to one another. For four of the smallest states, that do not collectively contain one-tenth part of the population of the United States, may obstruct the most salutary and necessary amendments....

What, sir, is the genius of democracy? Let me read that clause of the Bill of Rights of Virginia which relates to this: 3d cl. "That government is or ought to be instituted for the common benefit, protection, and security of the people, nation, or community; of all the various modes and forms of government, that is best which is capable of producing the greatest degree of happiness and safety, and is most effectually secured against the danger of mal-administration, and *that whenever any government shall be found inadequate, or contrary to these purposes, a majority of the community hath, an indubitable, unalienable, and indefeasible right to reform, alter or abolish it in such manner as shall be judged most conducive to the public weal.*" This, sir, is the language of democracy; that a majority of the community have a right to alter their government when found to be oppressive; but how different is the genius of your new constitution from this? How different from the sentiments of freemen, that a contemptible minority can prevent the good of the majority? If then gentlemen standing on this ground, are come to that point, that they are willing to bind themselves and their posterity to be oppressed, I am amazed and inexpressibly astonished.

From: *Patrick Henry: Life, Correspondence, and Speeches,* 3 vols., W. W. Henry, ed. (New York: Charles Scribner's Sons, 1891).

The Argument for a Constitution

Today, we view the Constitution as a sacred document. It is hard to imagine a time when Americans knew little of it and, in fact, were not even totally convinced of its usefulness. The truth is, however, that once the Constitution was written and adopted, much still had to be done. The document would not go into effect if at least 9 of the 13 original states did not approve, or "ratify," what the convention of 1787 had created. To push ratification, the delegates from the Constitutional Convention needed to go back to their states and essentially "sell" this new idea to the public.

As has already been noted, there was much debate at the Constitutional Convention over how America's new government should be structured. Many people, such as Patrick Henry, were strongly against the ideas outlined in the Constitution. Henry feared that too strong a central government would take too much power away from the people. Others worried that representation for the states would not be fair; they believed that the interests of the largest states would always overpower those of the smaller states.

Alexander Hamilton (1755–1804), James Madison, and John Jay (1745–1829) were some of the convention's most powerful supporters of the Constitution. They wanted to convince people throughout the 13 states that a constitution such as the one they had developed offered the fairest and the most ideal form of government.

The Federalist Papers was a series of 85 political essays written in 1787 and 1788. Although they were published under the pseudonym "Publius," the real authors were Alexander Hamilton, James Madison, and John Jay. Hamilton would later become secretary of the treasury in George Washington's administration, Madison would become the fourth president of the United States, and John Jay was later to serve as the first chief justice of the U.S. Supreme Court.

The essays were begun by Hamilton and were designed to persuade New Yorkers to approve the newly created Constitution. All but 8 of the essays first appeared in New York newspapers. Hamilton wrote 51 of the essays, Madison wrote 14, and Jay wrote 5. The authorship of the remaining 15 essays is in dispute,

The Constitution was signed by a majority of delegates at the Constitutional Convention by September 17, 1787. After its signing, it went to the states for ratification. Oil painting by Howard Chandler Christy (*Architect of the Capitol*).

James Madison. Oil painting by William Harding (*National Portrait Gallery*).

but most historians believe that they were written by either Hamilton or Madison.

The Federalist is now regarded as a classic work of political theory. The authors wrote about the many problems facing democracies, and they argued that the federal system recently created—one in which the national government and state governments share powers—was the best way to safeguard individual freedoms from tyrannical rule.

The excerpt printed here is from *The Federalist, No. 10*, which was written in 1787 by James Madison. In it, Madison describes the difference between a pure democracy—where people actually administer their government themselves—and a representative government—where people elect representatives to do the work of governing.

The Federalist, No. 10
James Madison

[A] pure democracy, by which I mean a society consisting of a small number of citizens, who assemble and administer the government in person, can admit of no cure for the mischiefs of faction. A common passion or interest will, in almost every case, be felt by a majority of the whole; a communication and concert results from the form of government itself; and there is nothing to check the inducements to sacrifice the weaker party or an obnoxious individual. Hence it is that such democracies have ever been spectacles of turbulence and contention; have ever been found incompatible with personal security or the rights of property; and have in general been as short in their lives as they have been violent in their deaths....

A republic, by which I mean a government in which the scheme of representation takes place, opens a different prospect, and promises the cure for which we are seeking. Let us examine the points in which it varies from pure democracy, and we shall comprehend both the nature of the cure and the efficacy which it must derive from the Union.

The two great points of difference between a democracy and a republic are: first, the delegation of the government, in the latter, to a small number of citizens elected by the rest; secondly, the greater number of citizens, and greater sphere of country, over which the latter may be extended.

The effect of the first difference is, on the one hand, to refine and enlarge the public views, by passing them through the medium of a chosen body of citizens, whose wisdom may best discern the true interest of their country and whose patriotism and love of justice will be least likely to sacrifice it to temporary or partial considerations. Under such a regulation, it may well happen that the public voice, pronounced by the representatives of the people, will be more consonant to the public good than if pronounced by the people themselves, convened for the purpose. On the other hand, the effect may be inverted. Men of factious tempers, of local prejudices, or of sinister designs, may, by intrigue, by corruption, or by other means, first obtain the suffrages, and then betray the interests, of the people.

From: *The Federalist Papers* by Publius (James Madison, Alexander Hamilton, and John Jay), published by various New York newspapers from 1787–1788.

CHAPTER 5

THE NATION GROWS AND LOOKS WESTWARD

Jefferson Expands the United States

In 1803, the United States paid France $15 million for 828,000 square miles of territory between the Mississippi River and the Rocky Mountains. This deal, called the Louisiana Purchase, brought under the control of the United States a vast, unexplored area that today makes up all of the states of Arkansas, Nebraska, Louisiana, Missouri, Iowa, and parts of Oklahoma, Kansas, Texas, Colorado, Wyoming, Montana, South Dakota, North Dakota, and Minnesota.

In 1800, Spain had secretly ceded this huge territory to France as part of a settlement between the two countries. The U.S. government was uneasy about having the French once again in control of land so close to the United States. France was an aggressive power at the time, and the settlers who lived east of the

Thomas Jefferson. Oil painting by Gilbert Stuart (*National Portrait Gallery*).

Mississippi were dependent on free access to the river for commerce.

President Thomas Jefferson instructed American minister to France, Robert Livingston (1746–1813), to discuss the purchase of the city of New Orleans and West Florida from the French. Unknown to the Americans, the French were seriously considering selling *all* the Louisiana Territory to the United States. French emperor Napoleon I (1769–1821) was preparing for war with Britain and felt that France could not defend such a huge land area against the British.

The French approached Livingston and his fellow negotiator, James Monroe (1758–1831), and offered to sell all the land. On April 30, 1803, the treaty was signed. Jefferson worried about the constitutionality of the purchase, but he was also concerned about

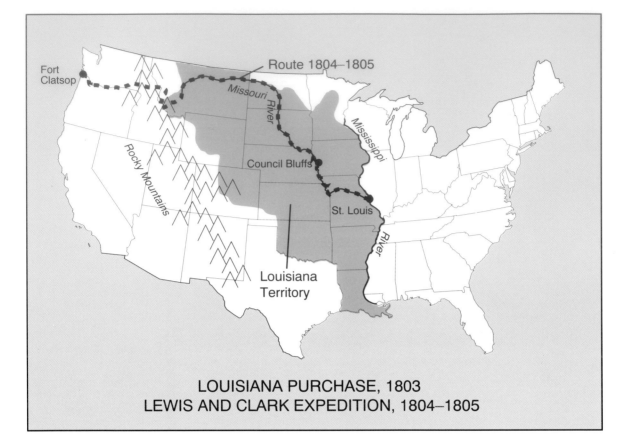

LOUISIANA PURCHASE, 1803
LEWIS AND CLARK EXPEDITION, 1804–1805

French power in North America. The American public approved the sale overwhelmingly, and the treaty was ratified by the U.S. Senate in October 1803.

Thus, with the stroke of a pen, the United States had doubled its size.

Having purchased such a vast new area of land, Jefferson was eager to have the territories explored. He requested an expedition that would report back to him on just what the new land offered.

To head the expedition, Jefferson selected his private secretary, Captain Meriwether Lewis (1774–1809). Lewis selected Captain William Clark (1770–1838) as his associate in command. In the winter of 1803–1804, the two men, and those joining their expedition, gathered in Illinois, and traveled across the Mississippi to St. Louis. In May 1804, they left St. Louis, traveling up the Missouri River. By the next winter they were camped near the Mandan Indian villages, near what is now Bismarck, North Dakota, where temperatures hovered at about 40 degrees below zero.

In 1805, the Lewis and Clark Expedition headed westward to the Rockies, the most difficult part of the journey. They were assisted by an Indian woman, Sacagawea, who served as a guide and helped them obtain the horses they needed to cross the mountains.

By the winter of 1805–1806 they had reached the Pacific coast in what is now Oregon. Here they built a fort called Fort Clatsop and spent a cold and rainy winter awaiting the return of warmer weather. By the spring of 1806, Lewis and Clark began their journey back toward Missouri. In July 1806, the party split up briefly in order to explore more territory. They were reunited in August and finally arrived in St. Louis on September 23, 1806.

The Lewis and Clark Expedition turned the interest of the American government and businesspeople to the territory west of the Mississippi. The explorers kept detailed records of every place they visited, and because of their systematic and efficient reporting, more expeditions were undertaken, and settlement of the region gradually began.

In the excerpt printed here from a letter to President Jefferson, Meriwether Lewis describes the many natural resources of the North American region, specifics on plant and animal species, and the various advantages that could be found for traders in this vast and undeveloped land.

The Lewis and Clark Journals

It is with pleasure that I announce to you the safe arrival of myself and party at 12 o'clock today at this place with our papers and baggage. In obedience to your orders we have penetrated the continent of North America to the Pacific Ocean, and sufficiently explored the interior of the country to affirm with confidence that we have discovered the most practicable route which does exist across the continent by means of the navigable branches of the Missouri and Columbia Rivers....

We view this passage across the continent as affording immense advantages to the fur trade, but fear that the advantages which it offers as a communication for the productions of the East Indies to the United States and thence to Europe will never be found equal on an extensive scale to that by way of the Cape of Good Hope; still we believe that many articles not bulky, brittle nor of a very perishable nature may be conveyed to the United States by this route with more facility and at less expense than by that at present practiced.

The Missouri and all its branches from the Cheyenne upwards abound more in beaver and common otter, than any other streams on earth, particularly that proportion of them lying within the Rocky Mountains. The furs of all this immense tract of country including such as may be collected on the upper portion of the River St. Peters, Red River, and the Assinniboin with the immense country watered by the Columbia, may be conveyed to the mouth of the Columbia by the 1st of August in each year and from thence be shipped to, and arrive in

Canton [China] earlier than the furs at present shipped from Montreal annually arrive in London. The British N. West Company of Canada were they permitted by the United States might also convey their furs collected in the Athabaske, on the Saskashawan, and south and west of Lake Winnipic by that route within the period before mentioned. The productions of nine-tenths of the most valuable fur country of America could be conveyed by the route proposed to the East Indies.

If the government will only aid, even in a very limited manner, the enterprise of her citizens I am fully convinced that we shall shortly derive the benefits of a most lucrative trade from this source, and that in the course of ten or twelve years a tour across the continent by the route mentioned will be undertaken by individuals with as little concern as a voyage across the Atlantic is at present....

I have prevailed on the great chief of the Mandan nation to accompany me to Washington; he is now with my friend and colleague Capt. Clark at this place, in good health and spirits, and very anxious to proceed....

The route by which I purpose traveling from hence to Washington is by way of Cahokia, Vincennes, Louisville, Ky., the Crab Orchard, Abington, Fincastle, Stanton and Charlottesville. Any letters directed to me at Louisville ten days after the receipt of this will most probably meet me at that place. I am very anxious to learn the state of my friends in Albemarle, particularly whether my mother is yet living. I am with every sentiment of esteem your Obt. and very Humble servant.

From: *Original Journals of the Lewis and Clark Expedition*, Vol. 7, Reuben Gold Thwaites, ed. (New York: Dodd, Mead, 1904).

This famous photograph of Dolley Madison is attributed to Mathew Brady. It was taken exactly one year before she died, in July of 1849. Although the image has been badly damaged, it is often reproduced because it is the only known photograph of Dolley Madison (*Library of Congress*).

A First Lady Remembers

Although women did not have the right to vote or own property in the early years of America's independence, they played a significant role in shaping the nation's destiny. Especially important were the wives of America's Founders, one of whom, Abigail Adams, had strong views on women's rights.

Dolley Madison, the wife of the fourth president of the United States, was a witness to most of the great events in the first 70 years of American independence. She was born Dolley Payne on May 20, 1768, in Guilford County, North Carolina, of Quaker parents. She was brought up in simplicity and in 1790 married John Todd, who died of yellow fever in 1793.

The next year Dolley married James Madison. In 1801, Thomas Jefferson became president and appointed Madison as secretary of state. Since Jefferson was a widower, Dolley Madison often acted as his hostess at the White House. Eight years later, Madison succeeded Jefferson, and Dolley finally was able to move into the White House as the First Lady.

When her husband became president, Dolley was only 40 years old. She was already known as a fun-loving and informal hostess, famous for her lively parties and dinners, and she maintained this reputation throughout her husband's presidency.

In 1812, the United States went to war with Great Britain, over territorial disputes and trading conflicts at sea. Two years after the War of 1812 began, the British invaded Washington and set fire to the White House. Dolley saved a number of important documents and a portrait of George Washington before fleeing the burning mansion. The White House was burned to the ground, and in the excerpt printed here from her memoirs, Dolley describes this dramatic moment in American history.

After leaving the White House in 1817, James and Dolley Madison retired to their home in Montpelier, Virginia, where they lived quietly until James Madison's death in 1836. In the years following her husband's death, the gracious and charming Dolley returned to Washington, where she once again gave parties and became a leader of society. Dolley Madison died on July 12, 1849, at the age of 81.

A Letter to Dolley Madison's Sister

[1814] Three o'clock.—Will you believe it, my sister? we have had a battle, or skirmish, near Bladensburg, and here I am still, within sound of the cannon! Mr. Madison comes not. May God protect us! Two messengers, covered with dust, come to bid me fly; but here I mean to wait for him.... At this late hour a wagon has been procured, and I have had it filled with plate and the most valuable portable articles, belonging to the house. Whether it will reach its destination, the "Bank of Maryland," or fall into the hands of British soldiery, events must determine. Our kind friend, Mr. Carroll, has come to hasten my departure, and in a very bad humor with me, because I insist on waiting until the large picture of General Washington is secured, and it requires to be unscrewed from the wall. This process was found too tedious for these perilous moments; I have ordered the frame to be broken, and the canvas taken out. It is done! and the precious portrait placed in the hands of two gentlemen of New York, for safe keeping. And now, dear sister, I must leave this house, or the retreating army will make me a prisoner in it by filling up the road I am directed to take. When I shall again write to you, or where I shall be tomorrow, I cannot tell!...

The memory of the burning of Washington cannot be obliterated. It can never be thought of by an American, and ought not to be thought of by an enlightened Englishman, except with deplorable shame and mortification. History cannot record it as a trophy of war for a great nation. The metropolis at that time had the aspect of a straggling village, interspersed here and there by a handsome public building, and with a scattered population of not more than eight thousand inhabitants; fortresses there were none, and but a few mounted cannon.

From: *Memoirs and Letters of Dolley Madison: Edited by Her Grand-Niece* by Lucia B. Cutts (Boston: Houghton Mifflin & Co., 1886).

Slavery in the Territories

The Louisiana Purchase of 1803 opened up a vast territory for westward expansion. As more and more settlers moved west, the country was forced to face an issue that threatened to tear it apart: Should slavery be allowed to expand into the new territories?

The country was bitterly divided along sectional lines on this issue. The South, where slavery was so vital to the economy and way of life, believed that settlers should be allowed to take their slaves with them and that slavery should be allowed to exist in the new territories. But most Northerners disagreed. Slavery was relatively insignificant to the economy of the North, and the North was also the home of much antislavery activity.

The issue was political, too. If a territory was admitted to the Union as a slave state, that would increase the power of the South in Congress. The reverse was true if a state came in as a nonslave state.

The Missouri Compromise of 1820–1821 was a series of acts that were first given great support by Speaker of the House and master orator, Henry Clay (1777–1852). They were passed by Congress to avoid the first major crisis about the extension of slavery. In 1819, Alabama was admitted to the Union as a slave state. With Alabama's admission, the number of slave states and nonslave states was exactly equal, and therefore so was the number of representatives of each in the Senate. When the Missouri Territory applied for statehood in 1820, it was anticipated that Missouri would be a slave state. The first compromise involved pairing the admission of Missouri with that of Maine, which would come into the Union as a nonslave state, thus preserving the balance in the Senate. The Missouri Territory was authorized to adopt a constitution that had no restrictions on slavery, but many Northern congressmen objected to a provision in the constitution that said that free blacks could not move to Missouri. As a result, another compromise was arranged. This time, a clause was added to the Missouri constitution that stated that nothing in that constitution would be considered an abridgement of the rights of free citizens, including free blacks. A third provision of the compromise prohibited the creation of any new slave states located north of the 36° 30' latitude, which was the southern border of Missouri.

Henry Clay was largely responsible for the adoption of the Missouri Compromise (*The Bettman Archive*).

The excerpt printed here is part of Section 9 of the Missouri Compromise, believed to have originally been written out by Senator Jesse B. Thomas of Illinois. In it, the senator describes the territory in which slavery would be outlawed and provides for the legal return of slaves who have escaped from slave states to nonslave states.

The Missouri Compromise, Section 9

And be it further enacted that in all that territory ceded by France to the United States, under the name of Louisiana, which lies north of Thirty-six degrees and Thirty minutes North latitude, excepting only such part thereof as is included within the limits of the state contemplated by this act. Slavery and involuntary servitude otherwise than in the punishment of crimes whereof the party shall have been duly convicted, shall be and is hereby forever prohibited: provided always, that any person escaping into the same, from whom labor or service is lawfully claimed in any State or Territory of the United States, such fugitive may be lawfully reclaimed and conveyed to the person claiming his or her labor or service as aforesaid.

From: Handwritten source by Senator Jesse B. Thomas; from the Records of the United States Senate, National Archives, 1820.

The Missouri Compromise was the first attempt to avoid sectional conflict over slavery. It held the peace for 34 years, when it was repealed and replaced by the Kansas-Nebraska Act in 1854. Although many people breathed a sigh of relief when the Missouri Compromise was passed, others knew that slavery would ultimately divide the new nation and lead to civil war.

FROM THE FRENCH AND INDIAN WARS, TO THE MISSOURI COMPROMISE: 1689–1821

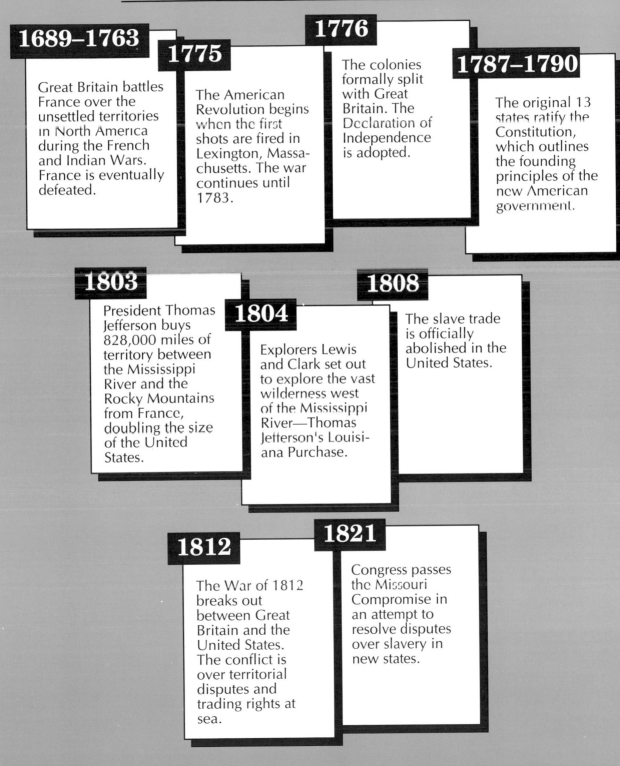

1689–1763
Great Britain battles France over the unsettled territories in North America during the French and Indian Wars. France is eventually defeated.

1775
The American Revolution begins when the first shots are fired in Lexington, Massachusetts. The war continues until 1783.

1776
The colonies formally split with Great Britain. The Declaration of Independence is adopted.

1787–1790
The original 13 states ratify the Constitution, which outlines the founding principles of the new American government.

1803
President Thomas Jefferson buys 828,000 miles of territory between the Mississippi River and the Rocky Mountains from France, doubling the size of the United States.

1804
Explorers Lewis and Clark set out to explore the vast wilderness west of the Mississippi River—Thomas Jefferson's Louisiana Purchase.

1808
The slave trade is officially abolished in the United States.

1812
The War of 1812 breaks out between Great Britain and the United States. The conflict is over territorial disputes and trading rights at sea.

1821
Congress passes the Missouri Compromise in an attempt to resolve disputes over slavery in new states.

FOR FURTHER READING

Brown, Marion M. *Sacagawea: Indian Interpreter to Lewis and Clark*. Chicago: Childrens Press, 1988.

Carter, Alden R. *The American Revolution: War for Independence*. New York: Franklin Watts, 1992.

Davis, Burke. *Black Heroes of the American Revolution*. San Diego, CA: Harcourt Brace Jovanovich Juvenile Books, 1992.

Dwyer, Frank. *John Adams*. New York: Chelsea House, 1989.

Keller, Mollie. *Alexander Hamilton*. New York: Franklin Watts, 1986.

Lindop, Edmund. *Birth of the Constitution*. Hillside, NJ: Enslow Publishers, 1987.

Nardo, Don. *The Indian Wars*. San Diego, CA: Lucent Books, 1991.

Osborne, Angela. *Abigail Adams*. New York: Chelsea House, 1989.

Osborne, Mary P. *George Washington: Leader of a New Nation*. New York: Dial Books for Young Readers, 1991.

Osborne, Mary P. *The Many Lives of Benjamin Franklin*. New York: Dial Books for Young Readers, 1990.

Petersen, David, and Coburn, Mark. *Meriwether Lewis and William Clark: Soldiers, Explorers, and Partners in History*. Chicago: Childrens Press, 1988.

Sandak, Cass R. *The Madisons*. New York: Crestwood House, 1992.

Vail, John. *Thomas Paine*. New York: Chelsea House, 1990.

INDEX